ON THE KLONDIKE TRAIL

by
Richard P. Emanuel

Cornelsen

On the Klondike Trail
Richard P. Emanuel

Technische Umsetzung
Jutta Debo

Umschlag
Peter Newark's American Pictures

Grafik
Kay Dixey, Linda Rogers Agency

Cornelsen online

http://www.cornelsen.de

1. Auflage € Druck 4 3 2 1 Jahr 04 03 02 01

Alle Drucke dieser Auflage sind inhaltlich unverändert und können im Unterricht nebeneinander verwendet werden.

Druck: Druck-Centrum Fürst, Berlin

ISBN 3-464-06846-3

Bestellnummer 68463

Gedruckt auf säurefreiem Papier,
umweltschonend hergestellt aus chlorfrei gebleichten Faserstoffen.

CONTENTS

CHAPTER ONE

Seattle – Gateway to the North

The sound of the voice in the kitchen told Willy Wolff that his Uncle Al was excited.

"I tell you, Karl, you never saw so much gold in all your life!" Albert Wolff said in a loud voice. He was talking with his older brother Karl, Willy's father.

"And it wasn't just dust. The man had a bag of gold nuggets the size of peas! No, bigger! I saw it myself. I was right next to him when he took out his gold and ordered drinks for everyone in the bar!"

Willy sneaked into the room just as his father filled the coffee cup on the table in front of Uncle Al.

"Slow down, Al," Willy's father said. "Some of the men at the fire station were talking about the big gold strike up in Canada, too. But it's hard to believe what people are saying."

"I thought so, too," Al said, "until I saw this guy's gold."

It seemed to Willy that everyone in Seattle was talking about gold. A week ago, on July 17, 1897, a ship had docked in Seattle with two tons of gold from the Klondike River, somewhere up north. Since then, people had been infected by a strange illness. Everyone called it "gold fever."

Uncle Al's eyes shone as he spoke. After a while, Willy saw that his father's eyes were shining, too.

"I'm going to the Klondike," Albert Wolff finally said. "I'm going to get rich, Karl. And you must come with me. We'll get rich together!"

Willy did not breathe while he waited for his father's answer. Suddenly, Karl Wolff noticed his son.

"Willy!" he said sharply. "How long have you been listening? Not one word of this to your mother or sisters, do you hear? This is just talk between Al and me. Now run outside and pull some weeds in the garden."

The door slammed behind Willy as he ran down the steps and into the garden. He stopped at a row of tomatoes. They were heavy with fruit. Willy's thoughts were spinning when he dropped to his knees and began to attack the weeds. After a few minutes, the sound of men's voices stopped and the soft voice of Karl's mother sailed through the window.

The back door slammed again as Uncle Al came out of the house. He stopped at the bottom of the steps to light his pipe, then walked along the path into the garden, towards his nephew. Willy jumped to his feet.

"Uncle Al," he said excitedly, "do you really think you'll find gold?"

"Can't fail, Willy," his uncle said. "The stuff is just lying on the ground up there. All you have to do is scoop it up! I only hope that your father comes along. Two can scoop up more gold than one."

"Uncle Al, three can scoop up more than two!" Willy said. "I want to go with you! I'll be 15 in a couple of weeks and I could be a big help. Will you talk with mother and father? Please!"

Albert Wolff smiled at his nephew. It seemed as if he had been Willy's age just yesterday. Like his nephew, Al had been a boy full of dreams and ideas. Now 30, Albert Wolff was a dreamer still. He puffed on his pipe.

When Willy walked into the kitchen with his arms full of tomatoes, he saw a scowl on his mother's face. Hanna Wolff was talking with her husband. Her voice was no longer soft.

"He's too young, Karl," she said. "Anyway, I need him here. You and Al can run off after gold if you want to, I can't stop you. But I'll need Willy to keep the store open. You know how busy it's been with this crazy gold fever. No, Karl, Willy must stay in Seattle with me."

It had been three years since the Wolffs had moved to Seattle. Eight years before that, in 1886, Karl and Hanna Wolff had said goodbye to their home in Clausthal, Germany. Willy had been just four when the family had arrived in the United States and he could not remember anything about Germany. His sister Lily, who was a year older than Willy, could not remember much either, but his other sister, Theresa, who had been eight, remembered the difficult move quite clearly and often spoke of what the family had left behind.

Life in the United States had been very hard at first. Karl Wolff learned English and worked at several jobs before he joined a railroad company. As the Great Northern Railway was built westward, the family moved west with the company. When the railway reached Seattle, on the Pacific Ocean, Karl took a job as a firefighter and life at last became a little more settled.

Hanna was a very good seamstress and had always made clothes for her family. She made rugged work clothes for Karl from heavy cloth and strong thread. Soon other firefighters asked her to make clothes for them, and Hanna began to sell clothes to make money for her family.

In Seattle, Hanna opened a shop. She made and sold work clothes to firefighters, ship builders and railroad workers. More and more miners came to Seattle to buy equipment for their mines in the wild northwestern mountains, and they too bought clothes from Hanna's company, which she called Wolff Wear. By 1897, Wolff Wear had a fine reputation, and Hanna made as much money from her special work clothes as Karl made as a firefighter.

Then gold fever hit Seattle.

Willy Wolff stood outside a busy store and looked at the heavy bags of flour in the back of Uncle Al's wagon. He looked at the packets of bacon which were piled next to him.

"Are you sure you will need all this?" he asked. "How will you ever get it all to the gold fields? Four hundred pounds of bacon! It might be easier to buy a pig and take it to the Klondike River."

Uncle Al laughed. "If we took a pig, we'd need food for the pig, Willy. And yes, we'll need it all! If we don't have enough equipment and food to feed two men for a year, the Mounted Police won't even let your father and me across the border into Canada. And Canada is where the gold is. Now help me load this onto the wagon. Then I want you to take it to my house. I have to buy some tools. I'll meet you in an hour back at the house!"

When the wagon was loaded, Uncle Al waved and disappeared into the crowd. Willy climbed into the wagon and picked up the reins. He shook the reins and the horse slowly began to pull the wagon towards home.

Shouts filled the air as Willy passed along streets which were piled high on both sides with supplies for the Klondike. Signs seemed to shout, too: "Miners' Supplies!" "Outfits for Alaska!"

Mountains had been made from bags of flour, sugar and beans. There were piles of tents and sleds, stoves, camping and cooking equipment of every description. Men, women and children walked or hurried through the streets. Others stood outside businesses to watch and discuss the activity or to swap the latest stories from the north.

At last Willy reached his uncle's home and began to unload the supplies. As he took things from the wagon, he checked them off on the list which his uncle had given him. At the top of the list were the words, "Outfit for Two Men". Under "Food", the list included 800 pounds of flour, 400 pounds of bacon, 200 pounds of beans, 200 pounds of sugar. There was coffee, butter, baking supplies, 100 cans of condensed milk, dried apples and other fruit. Under "Camping Equipment" there were blankets and tents, laundry soap and pots for cooking. The list of clothes included woolen socks, shirts and trousers, boots and raincoats. On the page for "Tools and Mining Supplies", Willy saw two words that made his heart jump. The words were written in large letters and underlined: "GOLD PANS."

Even with Willy's help, Karl and Al Wolff took two weeks to buy and pack their Klondike outfit. And every day, ships crowded with passengers sailed from Seattle for Alaska. Finally, the Wolff brothers were ready to join the stampede to the north.

The evening of August 8th, 1897, was strangely quiet in the Wolff house. The family met for a last dinner before Karl and Al began their adventure.

Hanna felt tired after working hard at her store. Thanks to the gold fever, she was selling work clothes as fast as she could make them. Still, Hanna had taken time to cook her husband's favorite meal: roast pork and potatoes followed by apple pie.

Willy ate little of his food. Lily sat next to her brother and tried to cheer him up. Across from Willy, Theresa talked and talked about everything but the one thing in everyone's thoughts: Karl and Al's departure in the morning.

When they were eating the pie, Uncle Al finally spoke. "Tomorrow is a special day," he began. "But perhaps you have all forgotten. It's Willy's birthday! He will be 15."

Willy sat up in his chair. He had forgotten his own birthday! Uncle Al put a small present on the table in front of his nephew. Lily clapped as Willy opened the gift.

"It's a pocket knife!" he shouted, as he turned the birthday present over and over in his hands.

"It's German. It's very well made," Al explained. "I got one just like it for me and one for your father, too. We'll use them a lot where we are going. And I guess you might need one too, if you follow your own gold rush someday."

He smiled at his nephew. Al didn't notice the scowl on Hanna's face. But Karl saw it. Willy saw it, too, but he looked away.

A soft rain fell in Seattle the following morning as Karl, Al and Willy Wolff drove their wagon towards the docks. They stopped on the dock next to the steamship *Excelsior*. The dock was crowded and so was the ship. It took almost an hour to load the Wolff brothers' outfit onto the *Excelsior*, which was getting ready to sail to Skagway, Alaska.

There were several ways to the Klondike but there was not enough time before Alaska's winter set in to take the longest route. That was the all-water route, which meant a 3,000-mile sea journey to the mouth of the Yukon River, then 1,500 miles up the Yukon to Dawson City, where the Klondike River joins the Yukon.

The Wolff brothers had decided to try a shorter route: They would sail north from Seattle to the town of Skagway. From there, two trails led through the mountains into Canada. The White Pass Trail led from Skagway through White Pass across rugged land to Lake Bennett. From there, a series of lakes and streams led to the Yukon River and down to Dawson City. The other trail began in Dyea, three miles northwest of Skagway, and ran through Chilkoot Pass to Lake Bennett and then on to the Klondike.

Karl and Al had discussed the two routes with anyone who had an idea. But they agreed that they would not decide which trail to take until they reached Skagway and could study things for themselves.

Willy helped his father and uncle settle on board the *Excelsior*. At 9 a.m., a loud whistle ordered everyone who was not a passenger to leave the ship. As he walked towards the gangway, Willy had a wild idea to hide on board the ship. Then his father gave him a hug, Uncle Al shook his hand and Willy joined the line of people walking down the gangway to the crowded dock below.

At 9:30, the *Excelsior* threw off the last rope and left the dock with another great blast of its whistle. Willy thought he saw Uncle Al wave goodbye as the ship moved away, but he could not see his father.

It was 11 a.m. when Willy climbed onto the wagon and shook the reins. His knife was in his pocket. He put his hand in his pocket and felt it. Suddenly he remembered what day it was.

"Happy birthday," he said to himself. He looked into the gray sky. The rain felt cold on his face.

CHAPTER TWO

North to Alaska

Willy Wolff's right hand slammed down hard on the kitchen table. His face was red as he shouted at his sister.

"Theresa, you should not talk about things you don't understand! And you know nothing about gold!"

"I know one thing," Theresa said with a smile. "Dad and Uncle Al won't find any gold. There are too many crazy stampeders like them who are trying to get to the Klondike. Dad and Uncle Al should have stayed here and helped mom, just as you are doing, William dear."

Theresa's smile made Willy suddenly explode with anger. He turned around and ran out of the house. He had to get away. He needed to think.

In the garden, Willy sat under a tree and pulled a letter from his pocket. Karl Wolff had written the letter to his son three weeks before, while he was sailing north on board the *Excelsior.*

Once again, Willy read his father's description of the ship crowded with stampeders. There were men from all over the world, and some women and children, too. Everyone was hungry for gold, excited and certain that he or she would soon be rich. But there was no one more excited or sure of his fortune than Willy's Uncle Al.

In Seattle, Willy had been busy with work since his father and uncle had left. He worked 16 hours a day at Wolff Wear and around the house and garden. But even while he worked, he could not think of anything else but the gold in the north.

At night, Willy dreamed of the Klondike River. With a golden shovel in his hands, he stood under a midnight sun and filled sacks with nuggets of gold. But every morning when he woke up, the dream slipped farther away. The great Klondike stampede was racing on without him.

Willy put his father's letter back in his pocket and walked out of the garden. He did not think about where he was going but he soon found himself on the docks. Two ships were unloading. One was the *Excelsior*!

An officer stood at the bottom of the *Excelsior's* gangway. Willy walked over to him.

"Excuse me, are you going back to Skagway? Do you need any more workers? I'm a hard worker!"

The man looked at Willy. "How old are you, son?" he asked.

Willy blushed. He paused. "I'm – I'm 17!"

The man was silent for a moment. "We do need workers," he said. "Half of the men that we hire jump ship in Skagway and don't sail back to Seattle. You wouldn't do that, now, would you, son? What's your name?"

"Willy Wolff, sir! No, sir! I just want to make some money."

"Well, we're leaving tomorrow morning and we can use a young man with some energy. Report to the galley. The cook's name is Erickson. Tell him you're the new kitchen boy."

It was long after midnight when Willy arrived back at his dark house. He lit a lamp in the kitchen and wrote a note to his mother. Then he wrote a longer letter to Lily. His mother would be angry, he knew, but Lily would understand. She had always been close to her brother.

"It will be hard at the store without me, Lily, and I'm really sorry about that," Willy wrote. "But business at Wolff Wear will start to slow pretty soon. Any stampeder who hasn't left Seattle by the end of August won't make it to the Klondike before winter. The problem is, Lily, if I wait until business slows, then I won't make it either."

It was true that Willy did not have a Klondike outfit, he wrote, but he could travel more quickly without one. He would catch up with his father and uncle and they had extra supplies. He would help them get to the Klondike faster. And he would help them dig more gold.

Willy loved his mother and sisters, even Theresa. But he was 15 now and he could not sit in Seattle and watch the stampede go by.

When he finished his letter, Willy went to his room and put some things into a cloth bag. At 5 a.m., he left the house.

There was fog in the street but the mist glowed with the first light of day. The light grew stronger as Willy walked block after block until somehow the glow began to slip into his heart. Willy began to whistle. He was on his way to the Klondike!

Doug Erickson, the chief cook on the *Excelsior*, whistled and sang while he worked. He was good to Willy but it was hot in the galley and dining room and the work was hard.

There were so many stampeders to feed that the dining room filled with people five times for every meal. When breakfast was done, it was time to serve lunch, and when lunch was finished, it was time to cook dinner.

Erickson watched Willy and seemed to know when he needed a break.

"Willy," he would call, "take some coffee to the captain!"

Bringing food and coffee to the wheelhouse was Willy's favorite job. He enjoyed getting away from the noise in the galley, and as he climbed the steep stairs, the wind on his face was cool.

The men in the wheelhouse did not say much to the young kitchen boy, but they let him look around. And there was much to see.

Dark green woods rose from the shore, sometimes close to the ship on both sides, sometimes far away across a shining, silver sea. Above the green woods, mountaintops covered with snow touched the sky. Blue-white glaciers flowed from the mountains down to the sea. Twice while Willy was in the wheelhouse, sailors shouted "Whale!" and pointed at the giant animals which were swimming near the ship.

At the end of the day, when the last pot was clean and Willy was completely exhausted, Erickson always took his young assistant to a small place behind the wheelhouse. It was never quiet aboard the *Excelsior*, where there were always some stampeders who were arguing and playing cards. But from the cook's secret place, the shouts were not so loud and the two friends could quietly talk as Alaska's awesome wilderness passed by.

By the fifth day, the cook had heard Willy's plan and he was worried.

"It won't be easy to find your dad and uncle," he said. "There are two routes to the Klondike from Skagway and you don't know which way they are going. You don't have an outfit and you can't get into Canada without supplies. And Skagway is a dangerous town, my boy. I wish you would sail back with us." But Willy was determined.

After a short stop in Juneau the next day, the ship traffic grew as the *Excelsior* neared the northern end of its route. When Skagway finally appeared, activity exploded aboard and around the ship.

Skagway was new and the town's one small dock was not large enough for the gold-rush traffic. Most ships anchored as near to shore as possible, then small boats crowded around to carry passengers and supplies to the beach. Stampeders shouted and pushed one another in their excitement to get into the boats. Sometimes, with a shout and a splash, a box or a passenger dropped into the sea.

Willy and Erickson rode to shore in a boat full of supplies for a restaurant in Skagway. The sailors who rowed the boat piled the supplies on the beach just out of reach of the water. Then they pushed the boat back into the sea, jumped in and rowed out for another load.

Erickson hired a wagon to carry the boxes of food to the restaurant. As Willy and the cook rode along the busy dirt street, Willy thought about his friend's words of concern.

There were hundreds of people – perhaps thousands – crowded into Skagway – and more were arriving every day.

Willy saw piles of lumber and heard the noise of hammers everywhere. Wooden buildings were going up all along the street, but it was still a town of white tents. Even the restaurant where they delivered their load of supplies was in a tent with a wooden floor. What Willy saw was a town that was being born on the edge of a great wilderness.

When their job was done, Willy and Erickson slowly walked back toward the beach. The older man put his hand on Willy's shoulder.

"Have you changed your mind?" he asked softly. "You won't get rich aboard the *Excelsior*, my boy, but you are sure to make some money."

Willy looked at his friend. He said nothing for a moment. Then he shook his head.

"No," he said. "I've come all this way and I am going to find my dad. He and Uncle Al can't be too far ahead of me." He tried to sound more certain than he felt.

Erickson sighed and reached into his pocket. He pulled out $50 and handed it to Willy.

"You will need this," he said. "It's your pay, plus a little more from me. I'm not supposed to give it to you until we start to sail back. The Captain thought you might want to jump ship. He was right, of course. But you've earned your money and it's wrong not to give it to you. Still, it won't last very long."

When they reached the beach, Erickson asked Willy for his mother's address in Seattle.

"I'll visit her," he said. "I'll tell her you are all right. And we'll meet again when you get home from the Klondike. You'll be rich, of course, but I hope you won't forget the poor old cook who sailed with you to Skagway."

The two laughed and shook hands. Then Erickson stepped into a boat.

"Good luck, son," he shouted. "Be careful!"

Willy waved and watched from the beach until Erickson's boat reached the *Excelsior*. Dark smoke rose from the ship and there were black clouds over the white mountains.

CHAPTER THREE

The Start of the Trail

The sun was still bright and the smell of the sea was in the air as Willy Wolff walked into Skagway. He slowly walked past stores which were selling groceries, equipment and clothes. He saw restaurants filled with hungry people and tents crowded with loud men who were drinking beer and playing cards.

In some places men stood in the street next to piles of supplies and argued about the price of carrying loads up the trails and into the mountains. Some men offered to carry supplies on their backs. Others offered horses for sale.

Willy looked around the busy street and wondered which way his father and uncle had gone. There were so many people passing through Skagway that he knew he would be very lucky to find someone who had seen and remembered the Wolff brothers. Perhaps if he learned more about the trails, he could guess which route his father and uncle had chosen.

Willy put his hand into his pocket and felt the $50 which Erickson had given him. It was more than he had earned, he knew. His friend had been kind. The money felt good in his hand and it made him feel brave. He also felt very hungry.

There was a tent nearby with a long line of men who were waiting to buy food. Something smelled good so Willy stepped into the tent. At the back of the tent a short man in a dirty white shirt was filling bowls with hot food. Behind the man was a sign with black letters that said, "BEEF STEW, BREAD, COFFEE – 50¢."

While Willy was reading the sign, a pair of loud men pushed into the tent behind him. One of the men ran into Willy and almost knocked him down. However, the man's friend grabbed Willy's arm from behind and pulled him back.

"Sorry, kid," the first man said. Then the two men left the tent and disappeared as quickly as they had appeared.

Five minutes later, Willy reached the front of the line. His stomach was making hungry noises. He reached into his pocket to pay for a bowl of stew. *His pocket was empty!*

A terrible feeling grew in Willy as he quickly searched all of his pockets. *Nothing!* All of his money was gone. The man who had run into him!

"Hey, kid," the man in line behind him roughly spoke. "Are you going to eat or not?"

Willy turned and looked wildly at the man. Then he ran out of the tent and down the street. He pushed people out of the way, not seeing where he was going. Suddenly, he crashed into a large man whom he couldn't push to the side.

"Hold on!" the man cried. He grabbed Willy's shoulders. "Where are you going, young man?"

He let go of Willy, who stepped back and wiped his eyes. Willy saw that the stranger was wearing a uniform, but it was not a uniform that he had seen before. The man saw the boy's confused expression and smiled.

"Colonel Sam Steele," he said, holding out a large hand. "Canadian Mounted Police. Now tell me, what's your name, son? And why are you in such a hurry?"

Half an hour later, Willy was sitting in a restaurant and talking quickly while he ate hungrily from a big bowl of stew. Colonel Steele drank coffee while he listened. His face looked serious.

"There's no question about it, Willy. It was the work of Soapy Smith's gang," Steele said. "Smith is the king of thieves in Skagway. He and his gang control this town. They steal from the stampeders in Skagway and along the trails into Canada. I came here to discuss the problem with the American police, but there aren't enough of them here to fight Soapy Smith. What happened to you is one of his gang's tricks. Smith's men often work in pairs. They probably followed you all the way from the beach after they saw your friend give you the money. They are probably dividing your money with Smith right now."

Willy looked up.

"What can I do, Colonel Steele?" he asked. "I'm in trouble without that money."

"I don't know how I can help you, Willy. I don't have any power outside of Canada," Steele said. "I wish I did. I'm sorry, but I don't think you will see your $50 again."

No one spoke for a moment. When Steele spoke again, his voice was soft.

"You aren't 17, are you Willy?" the Mountie asked. "That's all right, you don't have to answer. But it seems to me that your friend Erickson gave you some good advice. You made a lot of money on the trip up here. If it's money you want, you'll make more on the ships which sail between here and Seattle than most of these stampeders are going to find in the Klondike. I've been there, Willy. I know what I'm talking about."

Willy looked into his almost empty bowl. Steele went on.

"If you do decide to go after your dad, I think you should look for him on the Chilkoot Trail. Most people who are starting out now are trying to get through Chilkoot Pass. The route is very steep but it's shorter than the White Pass Trail. They hope to get as far as they can before the cold weather freezes the rivers and lakes. That will stop most travel until spring. Your uncle and dad could be on one or the other trail, of course. But I would guess they are on the Chilkoot."

Steele paused again to drink some coffee.

"One thing I will tell you, Willy: Don't stay in Skagway. There are dangers along the trail, but you will find people there who will help each other. Here in town, everyone is afraid of Soapy Smith. I've met lots of bad men in my work but Soapy Smith is one of the worst. There aren't many United States police officers here yet, and Smith and his gang control things. Until that changes, things in Skagway will only become more dangerous."

When he had finished his coffee, Colonel Sam Steele of the Mounted Police put five dollars on the table in front of Willy. He then stood up and walked outside. Willy followed. The two shook hands, wished each other luck and walked in different directions.

An hour later, Willy was sitting on a log and looking across the blue-gray water. A boat was coming toward the shore. It was the ferry between Skagway and Dyea, the town at the start of the Chilkoot Trail. The ferry was busy today. Willy watched as the boat tied up at the dock. A small group of passengers got off and walked into Skagway.

On the dock, a pretty girl about Willy's age and a young man who was a little older than Willy stood next to a large pile of supplies. They were talking with the ferry captain. The captain shook his head and began to argue.

"I can't carry it all in one trip," the ferry captain said. "You are not the only passengers and there is more cargo than just yours. You'll have to leave some of it here and come back for it."

"We can't leave the cargo here without someone to watch it," young man said angrily. "And if my sister stays here to watch it, who will watch the supplies in Dyea while I come back?"

Willy got off the log and walked toward the group.

"Can I help?" he asked. "I would be happy to watch your things. Are you taking all of this to Dyea?"

"Actually, we are taking it to Sheep Camp," the boy said. "That's 13 miles up the Chilkoot Trail."

"Our mother has a restaurant there," said the girl. "My name is Lucy Stewart and this is my brother, Jack."

"Hi. I'm Willy Wolff."

"We could use your help, Willy," said Jack. "And we can pay you. But how do we know we can trust you? We don't know you."

"You can take this with you," said Willy, as he gave Jack the cloth bag on his shoulder. "There isn't much in it but it is everything that I have."

"OK then. I'll give you $2 to watch our supplies while Lucy and I take the first load to Dyea," Jack said. "If you help us get it all the way to Sheep Camp, I'll give you another $8, plus the best meal you can get on the Chilkoot Trail!"

The three young people worked quickly to load half of their supplies onto the ferry. Jack shook hands with Willy, and Lucy smiled a warm smile. The three new friends waved at each other as the ferry left the dock and sailed across the dark water.

An hour later, with all the cargo in Dyea, Willy lifted a backpack filled with supplies onto his back. He took the reins of a horse that was also loaded with cargo and got in line behind Lucy. She was carrying a backpack that was only a little lighter than Willy's. She followed her brother, who was carrying the heaviest backpack and was also leading a horse.

Trail Street, the main route through Dyea, looked to Willy very much like Skagway. Rough, new wooden buildings stood next to white tents that flapped in the wind. There were hotels and restaurants and many stores with supplies for stampeders. Shouts of excitement filled the air.

North of Dyea, the trail followed the Taiya River, which flowed down from Chilkoot Pass. The first few miles of the trail were quite flat, and Willy, Lucy and Jack were strong. They soon reached Finnegan's Point, 4 miles from Dyea.

"The trail crosses the river here," Jack explained to Willy. "The Finnegan family has built a little wooden bridge. It costs a dollar for each of us to cross. Old Finnegan is making a lot of money with his bridge! But don't worry, I'll pay. There's a small camp on the other side. We can rest there and eat a little."

A few minutes later, Willy took a bite of an apple while Lucy cut bread and cheese for a snack. While they ate, Willy, Lucy and Jack told each other about their families.

The Stewarts were from Minnesota, where Lucy and Jack had been born on a farm. Their father had died in an accident two years ago, and after that, their mother could not run the farm. Mary Stewart and her children moved to Seattle, where Mary's older sister lived.

"But how did you get here?" Willy asked. "How did you get to the Chilkoot Trail?

"My mother and aunt both worked in a restaurant in Seattle," Jack explained. "My mother cooked and my aunt ordered supplies and ran the business. When the stampede started, they decided to open a restaurant in Skagway. But then we saw what Skagway is like. Do you know who Soapy Smith is?"

Willy nodded but said nothing.

"Well, they decided to move out onto the trail," Jack said. "Sheep Camp seemed like a good place for a restaurant, and ours is the best one there. It's called 'The Gold Nugget'."

"Our aunt got sick about a month ago," Lucy said. "She went back to Seattle. She's better now. My mother writes to her and she sends us food and supplies. She sent the things that we are carrying today. You'll see the restaurant tomorrow, Willy. Sheep Camp is a rough place but it is growing and changing fast. And it's really exciting to be a part of this stampede."

"Well, I'm glad you find it exciting, Lucy," Jack said with a smile. "Now let's get going! We'll camp at Canyon City tonight and finish our trip tomorrow."

The Chilkoot Trail slowly rose over the next few miles. Lucy and Willy talked as they walked. Willy learned that Lucy was 14, while her brother was 17. Jack wanted very much to follow the trail to the Klondike, Lucy said, but he couldn't leave his mother and younger sister alone in Sheep Camp.

In the late afternoon, Willy, Lucy and Jack reached the entrance to a small canyon. A little town had grown there, called Canyon city. They put up a tent on the edge of town and spent a quiet night of rest, talk and sleep.

The next morning, after breakfast, they loaded the horses and put on their backpacks once again. The trail became narrow and steep as it climbed through the canyon. Willy's backpack began to feel very heavy, but he didn't want Lucy or Jack to know.

At the top of the canyon, the three of them stopped and rested and admired the view of the mountains around them. The trail then rose gently for the last few miles that led to Sheep Camp.

When they reached town, the Gold Nugget restaurant was crowded with people eating lunch. Willy, Jack and Lucy

unloaded the horses and carried the supplies into the restaurant's store room. For the rest of the afternoon, the three young people worked in and around the Gold Nugget.

Dinner that night was as large and delicious as Jack had promised. The three new friends laughed and joked as they ate. After dinner, Jack gave Willy a blanket and helped him clear space in the store room where he could sleep.

As he relaxed on the floor, Willy thought about all that had happened since he had left Seattle. Here he was in Sheep Camp, halfway between Dyea and Chilkoot Pass. Of course, the rest of the trail to the pass was the steep and difficult part. He had little money and no outfit. He didn't know where his father and uncle were, or even which trail they were on.

Still, the last few days had been exciting. He had been unfortunate, because he had been robbed, but he had also been very lucky to meet Jack and Lucy. Willy smiled as he fell asleep. He dreamed that he was walking the Chilkoot Trail. In Willy's dream Lucy Stewart was walking next to him.

CHAPTER FOUR

Sheep Camp

It was dark outside when Willie woke up in the morning. He could hear the noise of pots and pans in the restaurant kitchen, next to the store room where he had slept. He got up and folded his blanket.

When Willy walked into the kitchen, Mary Stewart turned and smiled.

"Good morning," she said. "Did you sleep well?"

"Oh, yes, Ma'am," Willy answered.

"I hope you like pancakes," Mrs. Stewart said. She picked up a plate and a fork and gave them to Willy.

"Jack and Lucy are in the dining room," she said.

Jack was finishing a pancake when Willy walked into the room. On the table in front of Jack was a plate with a big pile of pancakes. Willy sat down beside Jack. The older boy put a fork into a large pancake and put the pancake on Willy's plate. Then he took another one for himself.

Lucy sat across the table from her brother.

"Good morning, Willy," she said. She poured a glass of milk and pushed it across the table toward their guest.

"Good morning, Lucy. Thanks, both of you," Willy said. "Say, what time is it?"

"Five o'clock. We let you sleep late," said Jack with a grin.

"The restaurant opens at 5:30," Lucy explained. "There will be a hungry crowd here soon."

Willy poured syrup on his pancake. He took a bite.

"This is delicious!" he said.

He asked the Stewarts about their life in Sheep Camp. Willy ate four pancakes while they talked.

Lucy told him she often worked in the kitchen and in the dining room with her mother. Jack worked in the dining room, too, but he also brought water from the Taiya River each day and did errands around Sheep Camp. Every two weeks, Jack went to Dyea or Skagway to get supplies. Lucy sometimes went with him.

"It takes a lot of work to run this restaurant," Lucy said. "After my aunt returned to Seattle, we hired a cook to help my mother. But the cook left last week. He had gold fever. He wanted to go to the Klondike. Now, I am afraid that mother is working too hard. I think she is getting tired."

"Who do you think is tired?" asked Mary Stewart as she walked into the dining room. She laughed and put her hand on Lily's head.

"Willy," she said, "Jack promised you $10 for your help. Here it is. What do you plan to do now?"

"I don't know, Ma'am," Willy said. "I really want to find my father and Uncle Al. But I'm not sure where to look."

"They might be on Bennett Lake," Lucy said. "Even if they went through White Pass, I would bet that's where they are now. There are thousands of stampeders camped on the lake. They are building boats so they can travel down the Yukon River to the Klondike. Most of them will be there all winter."

"Lucy is right," Jack agreed. "It is 500 miles by water from Bennett Lake to the Klondike but the lakes and streams will freeze soon. Most stampeders will have to wait until spring to go to the Klondike. If you can reach Bennett Lake before spring, perhaps you will find your father and uncle there."

"But I will need an outfit to get into Canada," Willy said. "How will I get one? Maybe I should get a job on a steamship again," he said. "I could earn some money and buy an outfit."

"If it's work that you want, why not work here?" Mary Stewart asked. "I will pay you $30 a week and give you meals and a place to sleep."

"You will make enough money to buy an outfit in a few months," Jack said. "You could be on Bennett Lake early next year. I'll help you to carry your supplies!"

"Me, too!" said Lucy. "We can help each other, Willy. And you can learn more about the trail while you work in Sheep Camp."

Willy looked at the three Stewarts. He grinned.

"I guess the Gold Nugget Restaurant has a new worker," he said. "What do you want me to do?"

"First, write a letter to your mother," Mrs. Stewart said. "She'll be worried. Tell her where you are. Tell her you are all right. Then get some water with Jack. And I'll need wood for the stove today. Lucy, I need your help in the kitchen. Let's get started, everyone!"

The weather had been sunny during the journey from Dyea to Sheep Camp, but the sky had become cloudy during the night. Now, it was raining.

Jack and Willy put on heavy rubber boots and stepped out of the restaurant onto the muddy trail.

"Let's get the water," said Jack.

The boys got a horse that was tied behind the restaurant. They attached a sled to the animal and put two empty barrels on the sled. Then Jack led the horse along the trail. Willy walked beside him.

They had seen many people on the trail from Dyea. Now, Willy was surprised to see how big Sheep Camp was.

Willy and Jack passed tents and wooden buildings that contained bakeries and stores. There were hotels and restaurants. There was a drug store and Willy saw a sign that pointed to a hospital.

Everywhere, people were walking through the mud and rain, and horses were pulling sleds loaded with supplies.

"There seem to be a lot of bars in Sheep Camp," Willy said.

"Yes," Jack agreed. "And they are always busy."

Jack stopped the horse when they came to a wooden platform beside the river. He took two buckets from the sled and tied ropes to them. He dropped one bucket into the river. Then he pulled the bucket up and poured the water into a barrel. Willy did the same and after a few minutes, the barrels were full.

When the boys got back, the Gold Nugget Restaurant was full of noisy customers. While Jack tied up the horse, Willy carried dishes into the kitchen. Then he helped Lucy wash them.

In the afternoon, Willy and Jack again took the horse and sled. This time they went to a little city of tents that was growing along the trail beyond Sheep Camp. Jack found two men who had firewood to sell. They loaded the sled with firewood and paid the men.

The rain had stopped and the sun returned as the boys traveled along the trail. Willy looked up at the mountains that rose up around Sheep Camp. The tops of the mountains were white with snow.

There was always plenty of work to do at the Gold Nugget Restaurant, but Willy liked it there. His favorite thing was talking with his friends. When he and Jack did errands, they often talked about the trail to the Klondike and all the gold they would find if they ever got there. When Willy and Lucy did the dishes together, they talked about their families and about the places they had lived and the places they would like to visit when the gold rush was over.

At night, after the restaurant closed, Willy, Lucy and Jack often played cards at a long table in the dining room. Sometimes Mrs. Stewart joined them, but most nights she was too tired. When they had finished their card games, if the weather was not bad, Willy and Lucy walked to the river. They would quietly talk together or just sit and watch the water. For Willy, these walks were the best part of the day.

One afternoon in December, Jack ran into the kitchen where Willy was washing dishes. It was snowing and Jack shook snow off his coat and boots.

"Willy, we're going up to Chilkoot Pass tomorrow!" he said. "Mother says we can go if we get water and firewood first."

"What are you talking about?" Willy asked.

"A man has just hired me to help carry his outfit to the summit," Jack explained. "He'll pay $5 to carry 75 pounds, and he'll hire you, too."

"Wonderful!" Willy said. "When do we start?"

"In the morning," said Jack. "But let's get the firewood tonight. It'll save time tomorrow."

Willy and Jack rose early the next day and went quietly outside. It was cold and dark. They led the horse and sled to the river. The river was frozen on top. They broke through the ice and filled two barrels with water.

After a quick breakfast, the boys walked to the Seattle Hotel. They found the man who had hired them in the hotel's restaurant. He was eating bacon and eggs and drinking coffee.

Mike Price was a tall man with a dark beard. They shook hands.

“Please call me Mike,” he said. “I’m glad you can help me. I’ve made ten trips to the summit already and I’m tired of going up and down.”

The sky was becoming pink when Willy, Jack and Mike began to hike up the trail. Each of them wore a heavy backpack.

“It is only four miles from Sheep Camp to Chilkoot Pass,” Mike said. “That doesn’t sound very far. The problem is, it’s also a half-mile up.”

Over the first three miles beyond Sheep Camp, the trail rose 1,600 feet as it went up to a small valley called the Scales, Mike explained.

“The last mile, from the Scales to the summit, the trail goes up another 1,000 feet,” he said.

“That’s what is called the Golden Stairs,” said Jack.

“That’s right,” said Mike. “That’s where you boys will really earn your money.”

One mile from Sheep Camp, the trail went around the front of a small glacier. Willy looked up the blue-white river of ice to where it disappeared into a cloud.

As the hikers climbed higher and higher, trees along the trail grew smaller and smaller. Soon the trees disappeared and the trail became a path of rocks and ice, which was surrounded on both sides by very deep snow.

At noon, Mike, Willy and Jack reached the valley of the Scales.

“It is called the Scales because people weigh their cargo here,” said Mike. “We’ll weigh our backpacks so I’ll know exactly how much to pay you. But first, let’s eat lunch.”

“I’d rather weigh the packs first,” Willy said with a grin. “I am going to eat so much that my pack will weigh only half as much after lunch.”

The valley of the Scales was crowded with stampeders. There were hundreds of people working to move outfits up the final 1,000 feet to Chilkoot Pass. On the valley floor, Willy saw scattered tents and a few wooden buildings. On the left side of the valley, a thin, dark line cut up across the white mountainside. It was a line of stampeders climbing the Golden Stairs.

Mike led the way to a tent that contained tables. He bought hot coffee and fresh bread for everyone. Willy poured milk and sugar into his cup and quickly drank his coffee.

"We have bread, cheese and apples," said Mike. "Who has a knife?"

Willy gave him his knife.

"This is a good knife," said Mike.

"It's German," said Willy. "I got it from my uncle. It was a birthday present."

After lunch, Mike led Willy and Jack to a wooden building to weigh their packs.

"Your pack weighs 72 pounds, Willy. I'll pay you $4.80 at the top," said Mike. "Jack, yours weighs 76 pounds. I'll pay you $5.20."

Ten minutes later, Mike stepped into the line of stampeders at the bottom of the Golden Stairs. Willy was behind him and Jack was behind Willy.

Before they had left Sheep Camp that morning, Mike had told the boys to bring strong sticks. Now as they climbed, they leaned on their sticks and pulled themselves up with each step.

In many places, the Golden Stairs really were narrow steps cut into the snow and ice. Everyone in the long line moved up the stairs at the same speed. If you were too slow, the stampeder behind you would shout. If you stepped out of the line to rest, most stampeders would not let you get back into the line.

When they were halfway up the Golden Stairs, a cold wind began to blow. Soon it started to snow. Willy could not see the top of the mountain. He could not see the valley below. He just looked at Mike's backpack and took one step after another. Willy's backpack seemed to grow heavier step by step.

After what felt like hours, Mike turned his head and said, "Almost there."

Suddenly, Willy's backpack felt a little lighter. The trail began to grow flat. Excited stampeders shouted to one another. After another fifty yards, Mike stepped to the side of the trail. He turned around.

"We made it, boys," he said. "Welcome to Chilkoot Pass!"

CHAPTER FIVE

On the Trail

Willy Wolff stood in deep snow at the summit of Chilkoot Pass. Scattered around him were tons of supplies, the outfits of hundreds of stampeders, all of which were covered with canvas to keep out the snow. The piles were marked with long sticks tied with pieces of cloth.

"We use flags so that we can find our outfits after snowstorms," Mike Price explained. "Storms always seem to blow through the pass."

Mike led the way to a pile marked by a green flag that flapped in the wind. He pulled a shovel from the pile and dug away two feet of snow. He emptied his backpack and added the new supplies to the pile. Willy and Jack did the same.

"I think you will like the trip down," Mike said. "It's a lot faster than the way up. But first, there is something I want you to see."

Mike led the way to where a crowd of men stood around a great pile of supplies.

"It's a kind of tram," Mike explained. "They just built it. You see, the rope goes around that big wheel and down to another wheel near the Scales. A horse turns the wheel and the rope carries things up. So now you can pay to have your outfit carried up by this tram! But I think it costs too much. They plan to build a bigger tram all the way from Canyon City to here."

The snow had stopped falling but Chilkoot Pass was windy and cold. Near the top of the Golden Stairs, Willy noticed a group of stampeders preparing to go back down the mountain. They were going to slide down in the snow!

Soon, Willy watched Mike wave and disappear down the mountain. Then Jack waved and slid after him. Willy sat down in the snow and slid after Jack. Their excited shouts echoed off the mountains.

During the next two weeks, Willy and Jack helped Mike carry the rest of his outfit to Chilkoot Pass whenever Mrs. Stewart and the winter weather allowed it. On New Year's Day, 1898, Mike entered Canada.

By the middle of January, Willy had earned enough money to buy his own outfit. Then he and Jack began to carry Willy's things to the summit whenever they could.

One sunny day in February, Jack stayed in Sheep Camp while Lucy hiked to the pass with Willy. The mountains that rose along the Chilkoot Trail looked especially wild and beautiful in the brilliant sunshine that morning.

Willy's outfit was almost all at the summit and he would soon be ready to enter Canada. He was eager to join the stampede for gold. He wanted to find his father and uncle. But Willy also knew that he would miss the Stewarts.

At the summit of Chilkoot Pass, Willy noticed some Mounties who were building a small wooden house for a checkpoint. He and Lucy talked with the Mounties, who gave them some hot tea to drink.

The ride down from the summit was the best ever for Willy. He and Lucy were both excited when they reached the Scales. With his heart beating fast, Willy put his arm around Lucy and gave her her first kiss.

Two weeks later, Willy, Lucy and Jack stood outside the Mounties' station on Chilkoot Pass. Willy's outfit had been checked. At last, he was ready to enter Canada.

Snow was falling and a cold wind blew through the pass, but the three friends did not hurry. They talked for a while. Finally, Willy and Jack shook hands.

"Thanks for your help," Willy said. "You are a good friend, Jack."

Willy gave Lucy a hug.

"I'll see you in Seattle," he said. "Remember what I told you."

"Hey, what does that mean?" Jack asked his sister.

Lucy did not answer. She just smiled and waved at Willy. "Be careful!" she said.

"I will," said Willy. "You too!"

Willy watched Jack and Lucy disappear down the mountain. Then he lifted a heavy backpack and turned toward the Klondike.

Beyond Chilkoot Pass, the trail quickly dropped down to the edge of a frozen lake. Then it went slowly downhill past two more lakes before it reached Lindeman Lake, eight miles from the pass.

The trail from the pass was rocky and frozen but around Lindeman Lake there was a forest. At the near end of the lake was the town of Lindeman. It was crowded with 2,000 stampeders. There were sawmills and wooden buildings and hundreds of tents in the town. Beyond Lindeman, the winter trail crossed the frozen lake.

Willy was tired, cold and hungry when he reached Lindeman. He went into a restaurant and ordered a dinner of beans, bacon and bread.

It was dark outside when he had finished eating. Oil lamps in the tents and buildings gave a weak light to the street. Willy found a small place to set up his tent on the edge of the frozen Lindemann Lake. He was still in his clothes when he got into his sleeping bag and he soon fell into an uneasy sleep.

When he woke in the morning, Willy was cold. He ate a quick breakfast. Then he found a man with horses and hired him to take him to Chilkoot Pass and return with the rest of his things.

With his outfit in Lindeman, Willy began to explore the town. He talked with the Mounties at their station and began to look for his father and uncle.

A week later, he was feeling depressed. He had supplies but his money would soon be gone. Where were his father and uncle? How could he find them?

One afternoon as Willy walked toward a sawmill on the edge of the lake, he heard a sudden shout. Men began to run towards the sawmill.

"Help!" he heard a voice call again. "My partner is under the logs!"

Behind the sawmill, Willy saw a man with blood on his face. There were logs on top of his legs. Other men were lifting the logs and Willy began to help. The man moaned in pain as they worked.

After 15 minutes the man was free. A doctor came and he told four men to carry the injured man to his surgery.

All afternoon Willy thought about what had he had seen. That evening he went back to the sawmill. A group of men was working to pile up the logs. Willy asked about the injured man.

"The doctor says he will live," a man with red hair told Willy. "But they had to amputate one of his legs. I guess the stampede is over for Bill. Maybe for me too. He was my partner."

Willy helped the other men pile the logs and then went back to his tent.

Two days later, Willy went to the post office to mail a letter to his mother. As he stepped out of the building, someone called his name. He turned. Mike Price was grinning and walking toward him.

"Willy! You made it!" Mike said. He shook Willy's hand with great energy. "When did you get to Lindeman?"

The friends went into a restaurant. They ordered apple pie and coffee and they talked.

Mike said he was moving his outfit to Bennett Lake. He planned to build a boat there.

"Bennett is a little closer to the gold, and every mile is important," Mike said. "When the ice melts, there is going to be a wild race down the Yukon River. It will be like no other race in history."

Willy told Mike about his search for his father and Uncle Al. Suddenly, Mike stopped him.

"Do you still have your knife, Willy?" he asked. "May I see it?"

Willy took out his knife and put it on the table.

"Do you mean this?" he asked.

Mike put a knife on the table, too. It looked exactly like Willy's.

"I got this knife in Bennett," Mike said. "A customer left it in a store by accident. I was shopping in the store and I found it. I ran after him but he had disappeared."

"Do you think it was Uncle Al?" Willy asked. "What did he look like? Mike, do you think he's still in Bennett?"

Two days later, Willy and Mike walked in front of a train of horses that carried their supplies to Bennett Lake. The sky was clear. The snowy mountains around them were brilliant in the sunshine.

The town of Bennett, on the edge of the lake, looked much like Lindeman. Willy saw thirty or forty new wooden buildings and hundreds of canvas tents. He saw several sawmills. The Mounted Police had a station in Bennett. And everywhere Willy looked – all around town and in camps around the lake – stampeders were building boats of all sizes and designs.

Mike and Willy unloaded their outfits at Mike's camp. Then they went to the store where Mike had found the German knife. Willy spoke to the store's owner. He described his father and uncle. But with such a busy store, the owner could not remember whether he had seen them or not.

“Why don’t you get a job in the store?” Mike asked. “You can watch for them while you are working.”

Willy asked the store owner if he needed another worker. At first, the owner was not interested. Willy then offered to work for little pay, and finally the owner agreed. Willy started to work at the store the next day. He sold rope and tools, shovels, axes and saws to crowds of customers. It was tiring work. Many stampeders were not pleasant customers, and Willy’s legs hurt as he had to stand all day.

One afternoon, Willy went into the store room to get a box of work clothes that had just arrived. He opened the box and found sturdy clothes just like those that he was wearing. He looked at the label inside the shirt: “Wolff Wear, Seattle USA.” Willy smiled. The clothes were from his mother’s business!

After more than two weeks in Bennett, Willy had not seen even one stampeder that he knew, except for Mike. Then one morning, he came in from the store room with a box of nails. He put the box on the floor and cut it open with his knife. Suddenly, he heard a voice that he knew.

Willy stood and looked at the man who had spoken. He was talking to the store owner.

“I need a knife,” the man said. “It is for my brother. He had a very good one but he lost it. Do you have any German knives?”

Willy stared at the man. For a moment, he did not move. Then he picked up his knife. He quickly walked across the floor.

“Do you mean like this?” he asked. He held out the knife in front of the man.

"Why, yes!" the man said. "Exactly like that..." His voice stopped. Karl Wolff turned and saw his son. Willy had a giant grin on his face.

"Hello, father!" Willy said.

"Willy! What are you doing here?" his father shouted. "How did you get here?"

"The same way you and Uncle Al did," Willy answered. "I came on the Chilkoot Trail."

CHAPTER SIX

Hanna

Spring came slowly to the Yukon River in May of 1898. The days grew longer, the birds began to sing again and flowers started to appear again, but the lakes and streams that poured their water into the Yukon River were still covered with ice.

In a small camp on Bennett Lake, Albert Wolff walked up and down along the frozen shore. Karl Wolff and Mike Price sat next to a fire on the beach. Near them, a small boat full of supplies sat on logs. It was named *Hanna* and it was ready to be pushed into the water as soon as the ice melted.

"Al, come and have some coffee!" Karl Wolff called to his younger brother. "The ice won't melt any faster just because you're watching it."

The three men were still drinking coffee when Willy Wolff arrived.

"I've just visited the Mounties," he said. "Colonel Steele says that the ice is very thin now. He thinks it will break in a few more days."

Albert took out his pipe and filled it with tobacco.

"I'll tell you the truth, Willy," he said. "Either the ice will break soon or your Uncle Al will. I just hope the ice breaks first."

Albert puffed on his pipe while the others laughed.

Two days later, on May 29, the ice on Lindeman and Bennett Lakes began to break apart. Water flowed through the lakes and poured into the Yukon River, carrying the broken ice along with it.

More than 7,000 boats of every possible design followed the ice down the river. Thousands of stampeders and millions of pounds of supplies were crowded onto the boats. The long winter had held the stampeders back. Now they flowed toward the gold fields in a fantastic spring flood. The great boat race to the Klondike had begun. And *Hanna* was in the race!

Willy and the others aboard *Hanna* were excited that they were moving toward the gold again but the trip was still hard work. They all took turns at the jobs on the boat: one man watched from the front of the boat while one worked the rudder and two pulled the oars. When the wind was strong, they put up a sail for some extra help. They slept very little.

The man in the front of the boat watched carefully for rocks and for other boats. Some of the stampeders around them traveled in small canoes and these were often hard to see. Others traveled on large boats loaded with dogs, horses and cargo, and these slow boats sometimes got in the way.

On the third afternoon, Willy was sitting in the back of the boat. The tops of the mountains along the river were covered with snow which glowed in the sunshine.

Suddenly Karl Wolff shouted, "Rock ahead, Willy! Left! Go left!"

Willy jumped up and pushed hard on the rudder. *Hanna* turned quickly. A moment later, the boat passed a large, dark rock.

"That was close," said Mike Price as he pulled on an oar. "Well done, Willy."

Willy and the others had already seen many boats get damaged or destroyed on the river. Some had crashed into other boats. Others had crashed into rocks and broken apart. The journey was most dangerous in the canyons where the river was narrow and fast and rocky, and where so many boats were trying to get through in a hurry.

A few days later, the evening sky was dark when *Hanna* reached a crowd of boats waiting at the entrance to a long canyon. A group of Mounties stopped all boats on the river to check them before they entered the canyon.

"It is dangerous for the next five miles," a young Mountie told the stampeders. "More than one hundred boats have already been destroyed here and five men have been killed. Women and children must walk around the canyon – there is a trail over there. How old are you, son?" he asked Willy.

The Mountie checked *Hanna* and asked questions about the men's experience with boats and rivers. Then he said *Hanna* could go – but not Willy. He was too young. He would have to walk.

Willy began to argue but his father stopped him.

"I'm sorry, Willy, but the Mountie is right," Karl said. "We'll see you on the other side."

Willy said nothing. He pushed some things into a backpack and walked away. He felt angry and disappointed. He followed a trail that climbed to the top of the dark gray rock on the side of the canyon. When he looked down into the canyon a few minutes later, his feelings turned from anger into worry.

In the canyon below, Willy saw a man in a canoe going very fast around rocks until he disappeared around a bend in the river. Following the canoe was a large boat with five men. It hit a rock and began to spin. It started to turn over and by the time it had disappeared around the turn, the boat was upside-down in the river.

Willy looked back and saw *Hanna* in a long line of boats. It would be two or three hours before it would be *Hanna*'s turn to go into the canyon. Willy decided to wait and watch for his boat at the end of the canyon.

When he reached the end of the canyon, what Willy saw made him worry even more. Beyond the canyon, on both sides of the river, he saw boats that had been pulled out of the water. Many had been badly damaged, some had been broken into pieces. Wood and wet supplies were piled everywhere.

Willy sat down to watch the boats as they came out of the canyon. Some floated out carrying men who were shouting with excitement. Many of these kept going down the river without stopping. Others stopped to pick up women and children before they pushed into the river again.

Other boats floated out broken or even upside-down. Sometimes stampeders were swimming next to their damaged boats.

After a long wait, Willy saw a boat that he had seen near *Hanna*. He stood up. Next came a canoe which moved around the last big rock and floated down the river. Then came a big boat. It was spinning when it appeared. It crashed into the final rock and got stuck! The three men in the boat were thrown into the water and swam away. A minute later, *Hanna* appeared.

Willy saw that their boat had come through the canyon without any damage. Willy's father stood at the rudder while Albert and Mike pulled the oars and tried to look ahead. They shouted to each other about whatever they saw.

Albert was the first to see danger ahead. Willy could see him shout. Soon all three of them shouted and *Hanna* quickly turned to the right. But it was too late.

Hanna's side crashed into the front of the boat that was stuck on the rock and suddenly both boats were spinning down the river. The first boat quickly broke into two pieces and sank. Then *Hanna*'s front hit the wreck and the boat turned upside-down.

Willy ran down the trail to the river. He saw other stampeders help pull his father and Mike to the shore, but Uncle Al was further down river. He was holding onto the upside-down boat and trying to push it toward the shore. Willy ran and jumped into the river. He swam to his uncle's side. Together they kicked and pushed and pulled the damaged boat to the shore.

"We still have most of the food," Mike said an hour later. "A lot of the camping equipment and most of the tools are gone."

"And we are all alive," Karl said quietly. "No one is badly hurt. Perhaps we can borrow some tools and fix *Hanna* well enough to go down the river. The Mounties said there is nothing as bad as this canyon the rest of the way to Dawson."

"We either go on to Dawson or we go back to Skagway," Mike said. "What do you say, Willy? Which way should we go?"

The boy said nothing but pointed down the river toward Dawson.

Albert grinned and hit Willy's shoulder. "That's my nephew!" he shouted.

"All right," Karl said. "We go on then!"

CHAPTER SEVEN

Willy's Gold

Five months later, on a sunny afternoon in October, the Wolff house in Seattle was filled with conversation.

In the living room, Karl and Albert Wolff and Mike Price drank beer while they answered Jack Stewart's questions about the boat race to the Klondike. They told him stories about the famous gold fields, and Jack told them about Sheep Camp and the Gold Nugget Restaurant.

In the kitchen, Mary Stewart and her sister helped Hanna Wolff and her daughters take pies out of the oven. Then they put in ham, potatoes and chicken. Willy and Lucy tried to help but the kitchen was too crowded. Willy's mother soon sent them outside.

In the autumn garden, Willy took Lucy's hand and led her to his favorite tree. They sat beneath the tree and talked about all that had happened to them since they had said goodbye on Chilkoot Pass.

"Our business did quite well after you left Sheep Camp, Willy," Lucy began. "The restaurant was very busy all spring but there were not as many customers by the end of the summer. Did you know that they are building a railroad from Skagway to Bennett Lake? Mother says that after the railroad opens, there will be no more stampeders on the Chilkoot Trail. We decided to sell the Gold Nugget Restaurant in September. We came back to Seattle with more than $20,000!"

"Lucy, that's wonderful!" Willy said. "You did better than we did in the Klondike. We were just too late. When we got to Dawson, we found that the best places to mine gold had already been taken. Most of the best places were taken before we had even left Seattle! Oh, some of the late stampeders got lucky. But most of us earned money by working in other people's mines. I made almost $1,200 working in gold mines during the summer. Then I spent some of it on the trip home."

Lucy and Willy talked for the rest of the afternoon. At six o'clock, Hanna called them inside for dinner.

The dining room of the Wolff house seemed to Willy almost as crowded and noisy as the Gold Nugget Restaurant. When the food had been set on the table, Hanna Wolff stood and asked everyone to be quiet.

"This celebration is to welcome everyone back – our new friends and especially our family members – from all their adventures," Hanna said. "We are happy that you are all with us today, and that you are all safe in Seattle."

As the dinner continued, the conversation and jokes grew louder and louder. Karl told the story of Tom Lippy, a young man from Seattle who brought home a suitcase with 200 pounds of gold from the Klondike.

"It is true that Tom Lippy got very rich," said Hanna with a smile. "So did some of the others who reached the gold fields early. But some of us who stayed home made money from the stampeders. Running away to dig up the ground somewhere is not the only way to make money."

"Why, you could also run a restaurant like we did!" said Jack. "Even stampeders have to eat."

"And they need clothes," said Karl. "Hanna, you are right. And I'm very glad that you and the girls were smart enough to stay home to make and sell clothes to all of us crazy stampeders. Wolff Wear has grown. You have built a very good business. I am proud of you."

"Yes, but the adventure!" Albert shouted. "No one can say how much the adventure was worth! I just got a letter from a friend of mine in Dawson. He is going to Nome, Alaska, to look for gold. And I might join him. Who will go with me? Mike? Jack? How about you, Willy? There is plenty of gold in Alaska, I tell you. And this time, we'll find gold!"

Everyone at the table laughed long and loud. After a moment, Albert laughed, too.

"No thanks, Uncle Al," Willy said. "We did have a great adventure. But I don't need to go to Nome. I found my gold on the Chilkoot Trail."

He took Lucy's hand.

"I found all the gold I need."

AFTERWORD

Gold was found along the Klondike River in western Canada in August, 1896. The next July, two ships with about 80 miners and more than $3 million in gold from the Klondike docked in the cities of San Francisco and Seattle.

The Klondike gold strike started a stampede to the gold fields of the far north. Most stampeders were American men but there were people from all around the world on the trails, including many women and children.

In the end, almost 40,000 stampeders reached Dawson. Most of them, like Willy Wolff, arrived too late to get rich. About 4,000 miners found gold. A few hundred did get rich. Most who went to the Klondike returned home with little money but memories of a great adventure.

The Klondike stampede changed western Canada and Alaska. In July, 1899, a railroad was built to Bennett Lake. In 1900, the railroad reached the Yukon River itself. A traveler could take a steamship to Skagway, ride the train to the Yukon River and get on a small steamer to travel 1,800 miles down the Yukon River to the sea. Such a trip by train and steamer would have seemed fantastic to the many thousands of stampeders who struggled up the Golden Stairs and through Chilkoot Pass during the winter of 1897-1898.

Tom Lippy, Soapy Smith and Colonel Sam Steele are historic figures. All other figures in *On the Klondike Trail* are works of imagination.

You can find more information about the Klondike Stampede on the Internet (e.g. tqjunior.thinkquest.org/5181, www.nps.gov/klgo or parkscan.harbour.com/khs).

VOCABULARY

Abbreviations

adv	=	adverb
jdm.	=	jemandem
jdn.	=	jemanden
n	=	noun
pl	=	plural
sb.	=	somebody
sth.	=	something

A

aboard [ə'bɔːrd] an Bord
actually ['æktʃuəli] genau gesagt
(to) **admire** [əd'maɪər] bewundern
advice [əd'vaɪs] Rat
ahead [ə'hed] voraus, nach vorne
(to) **amputate** amputieren
(to) **anchor** ['æŋkər] ankern
anger ['æŋgər] Wut
(to) **argue** ['aːrgjuː] sich streiten
(to) **attach** [ə'tætʃ] festmachen
axe [æks] Axt

B

baking supplies [sə'plaɪz] Backvorräte
barrel Fass
bean Bohne
beard ['biːərd] Bart
(to) **beat** schlagen
bend Kurve
boot Stiefel
(to) **borrow** sich leihen
bowl [boʊl] Schüssel
bucket Eimer

C

canvas ['kænvəs] Leinwand
cargo Schiffsladung
(to) **catch up with** einholen
(to) **change your mind** deine Meinung ändern
(to) **clear** freiräumen
(to) **climb** [klaɪm] ansteigen
condensed milk Kondensmilch
confused [kən'fjuːzd] verwirrt
(to) **contain** enthalten
(to) **control** unter Kontrolle haben, in der Hand haben
crowd [kraʊd] Menge (von Leuten)
crowded with voller

D

damaged ['dæmɪdʒd] beschädigt
delicious [dɪ'lɪʃəs] köstlich
(to) **deliver** [dɪ'lɪvər] liefern
departure [dɪ'pɑːrtʃər] Abreise
depressed deprimiert
determined [dɪ'tɜːrmɪnd] entschieden, bestimmt
disappointed enttäuscht
(to) **dock** anlegen
downhill bergab
drug store Drugstore, Drogerie, Apotheke
dust Staub

E
(to) **earn** [ɜːrn] verdienen
(to) **enter (a country)** in (ein Land) einreisen
errand ['erənd] Besorgung, Auftrag
especially [ɪ'speʃəli] besonders
experience [ɪk'spɪriens] Erfahrung
(to) **explode with anger** ['æŋgə] vor Wut platzen

F
fever Fieber
firefighter Feuerwehrmann
firewood Brennholz
(to) **flap** flattern
(to) **float out** [floʊt] heraustreiben
flood [flʌd] Flut
flour ['flaʊər] Mehl
(to) **flow** fließen; sich schieben
fog Nebel
fortune ['fɔːrtʃuːn] Glück
fresh frisch
front Anfang; Spitze, Bug

G
galley Kombüse, Schiffsküche
gang Bande
gangway Laufplanke
gently [dʒentl] (adv) sanft
glacier ['gleɪʃər] Gletscher
(to) **glow** glänzen, leuchten
(to) **grab** greifen
grin (n) Grinsen
(to) **grin** grinsen
groceries ['grəʊsəriːz] (pl) Lebensmittel

H
halfway auf halber Strecke
(to) **hand sth. to sb.** jdm. etwas geben
(to) **hide** sich verstecken
(to) **hire** ['haɪər] einstellen
(to) **give sb. a hug** [hʌg] jdn. umarmen
hurry (n) Eile
(to) **hurry** sich beeilen, laufen

J
(to) **join (a company)** [dʒɔɪn] bei (einer Firma) anfangen
(to) **jump ship** das Schiff vorzeitig verlassen

K
(to) **knock down** zu Boden werfen

L
(to) **last** reichen
(to) **lean** lehnen
load [loʊd] (n) Ladung
(to) **load** [loʊd] laden, beladen
log Baumstamm
lumber ['lʌmbər] Bauholz

M
Ma'am gnädige Frau
(to) **mine** schürfen
miner Bergarbeiter
mountaintop Gipfel
Mounted Police kanadischer berittene Polizei
Mountie berittener Polizist

N
nearby [ˌnɪr'baɪ] in der Nähe
nephew ['nefjuː] Neffe
nugget ['nʌgɪt] Klumpen

O
oar [ɔːr] Riemen, Ruder
once again noch einmal

P

pan Pfanne
pancake Pfannkuchen, Eierkuchen
pass Pass(straße)
(to) **pass through (a place)** durch (ein Ort) durchreisen
(to) **pause** [pɔːz] innehalten
pay Lohn
apple pie [paɪ] gedeckter Apfelkuchen
(to) **pile (up)** aufhäufen
platform Plattform
plenty of eine Menge
pound Pfund
pretty ziemlich
(to) **puff** paffen

R

(to) **race on** weitergehen
raincoat Regenmantel
(to) **reach** greifen
out of reach [riːtʃ] außer Reichweite
rein [reɪn] Zügel
(to) **report** sich melden
roast pork Schweinebraten
rocky felsig
rough [rʌf] grob
(to) **row** [roʊ] rudern
rudder Steuerruder
rugged ['rʌgɪd] grob, rau; wild, felsig
(to) **run into sb.** gegen jdn. rennen

S

sail Segel
sale Verkauf
sawmill Sägewerk
scales Waage
scattered verstreut
(to) **scoop** [skuːp] schaufeln
scowl [skaʊl] böser Ausdruck
seamstress ['siːmstrəs] Näherin
series ['sɪriːz] Reihe, Folge
(to) **serve** [sɜːrv] servieren
(to) **set in** beginnen
settle sich einleben, sich eingewöhnen
settled geregelt
shore [ʃɔːr] Küste
shoulder Schulter
shout (n) Schrei
(to) **shout** schreien
shovel ['ʃʌvl] Schaufel
(to) **sigh** [saɪ] seufzen
silver silbern
(to) **slam** zuschlagen
(to) **slide down** hinunterrutschen
(to) **slip away** dahinschwinden
smell Geruch
snowstorm Schneesturm
space Platz
(to) **spin** herumwirbeln
splash Platschen
stampede [stæm'piːd] Ansturm
(to) **stare at** anstarren
(to) **steal** stehlen
steamship Dampfschiff
steep steil
(to) **step into sth.** in etwas treten
(to) **step back** zurücktreten
stew [stjuː] Eintopf
store room Lagerraum
stove [stoʊv] Herd, Kocher
strike Fund
suitcase ['suːtkeɪs] Koffer
summit ['sʌmɪt] Gipfel
supplies [sə'plaɪz] (pl) Vorrat
(to) **be not supposed to do sth.** etwas nicht machen dürfen

surgery ['sɜːrdʒəri] Sprechzimmer
(to) **surround** [sə'raʊnd] umgeben
syrup ['sɪrəp] Sirup

T
thread [θred] Garn, Faden
(to) **tie up** festmachen
tiring ermüdend
ton Tonne
trail [treɪl] Weg, Pfad
(to) **turn over** kentern, umkippen

U
(to) **unload** [ʌn'loʊd] ausladen

W
wagon (Plan)Wagen
(to) **wave** winken
weak schwach
weed Unkraut
(to) **weigh** [weɪ] (ab)wiegen
wheelhouse Steuerhaus
whistle ['wɪsl] Pfeifen
wilderness Wildnis
(to) **wipe** reiben
wooden Holz-
(to) **be worth** wert sein
wreck [rek] Wrack

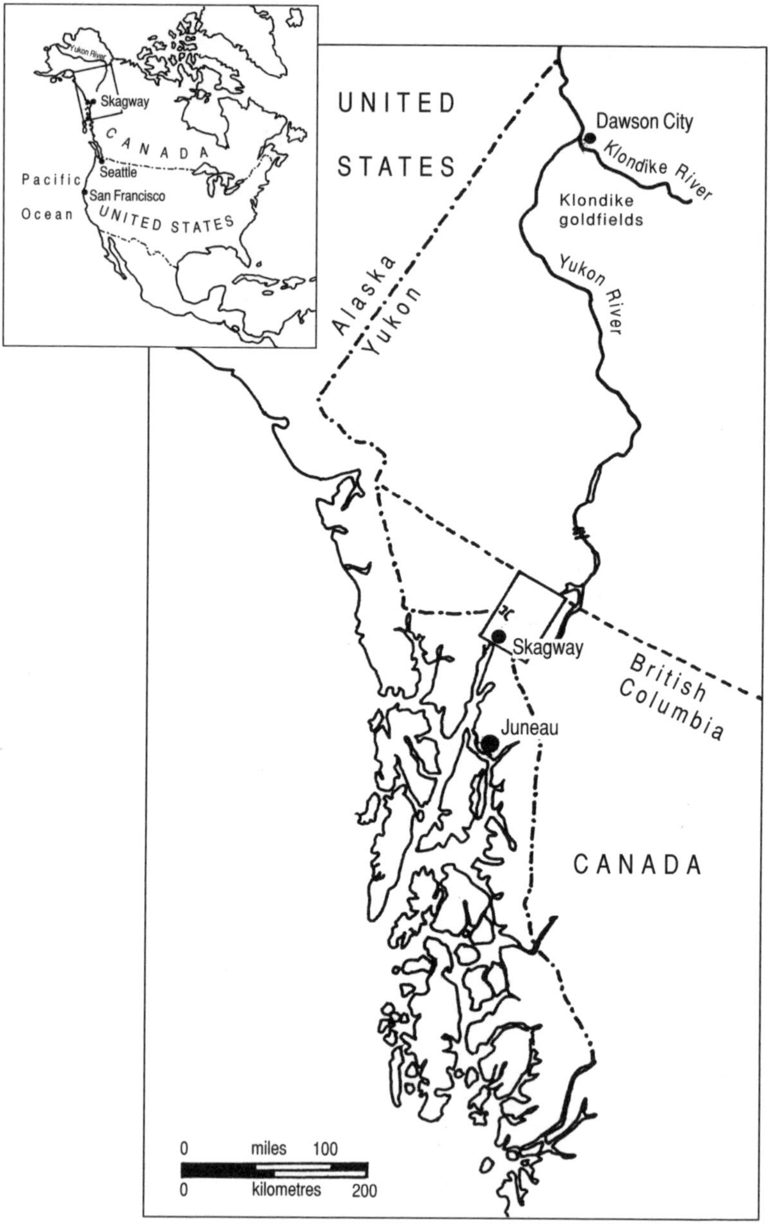

Yukon River
Skagway
CANADA
Pacific
Ocean
Seattle
San Francisco
UNITED STATES
UNITED
STATES
Dawson City
Klondike River
Klondike
goldfields
Yukon River
Alaska
Yukon
Skagway
British
Columbia
Juneau
CANADA
0
miles
100
0
kilometres
200

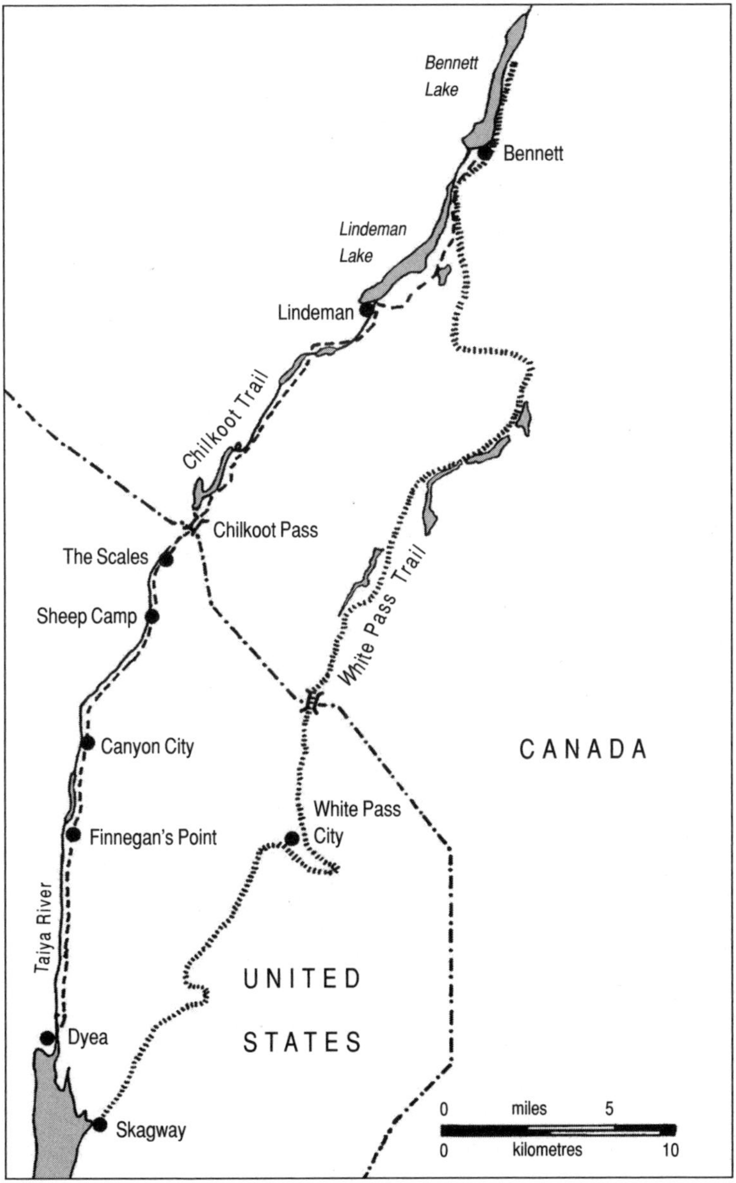
Bennett Lake
Bennett
Lindeman Lake
Lindeman
Chilkoot Trail
Chilkoot Pass
The Scales
Sheep Camp
White Pass Trail
Canyon City
CANADA
White Pass City
Finnegan's Point
Taiya River
UNITED STATES
Dyea
Skagway
0 miles 5
0 kilometres 10